SOLO FORMS is an innovative approach to the formal exercises of karate, aikido, tai chi and kung fu.

STUDENTS and enthusiasts working alone, without partners, will find a wide range of solo routines they can practice for exercise and fitness, for personal development, and for the sheer pleasure of the activity.

INSTRUCTORS can use this book as a visual aid in the teaching of form work. Physical education teachers will find this text especially appropriate for young people; the sole aim is noncompetitive self-development without body contact.

EIGHT DIFFERENT forms are explained step-by-step and illustrated with more than 400 photos. Included are two staff (long stick) routines and a brilliant free-form improvisation to stimulate interest in self-expression through creative movement.

YA *"...formal and improvised (routines) that can be used for personal enjoyment and exercise ... a useful tool for the individual or instructor."*

"...well-coordinated, step-by-step instructions and photos lead the individual through various solo routines... "

American Library Association **BOOKLIST**

SOLO FORMS

of KARATE, TAI CHI, AIKIDO & KUNG FU

BRUCE TEGNER & ALICE McGRATH

THOR PUBLISHING COMPANY

VENTURA   CA.   93002

Library of Congress Cataloging in Publication Data

Tegner, Bruce.
    Solo forms of karate, tai chi, aikido, and kung fu.

    Includes index.
    Summary: Describes nine non-contact, non-competitive
routines from various oriental martial arts which can be performed
by a single individual for the purpose of exercising and conditioning
the body.
       1. Exercise. 2. Hand-to-hand fighting, Oriental.
[1. Exercise. 2. Hand-to-hand fighting, Oriental]
I. McGrath, Alice Greenfield, 1917-   . II. Title.

GV505.T43   613.7'1   81-1745
ISBN 0-87407-034-1 (pbk.)   AACR2

SOLO FORMS of
Karate, Tai Chi, Aikido & Kung Fu

THOR PUBLISHING COMPANY
P.O. BOX 1782
VENTURA, CA 93002   *Printed in U.S.A.*

BRUCE TEGNER BOOKS REVIEWED

KARATE: BEGINNER to BLACK BELT
"Techniques and routines...illustrated in profuse detail...a fine
introduction and a worthwhile reference source...specially geared
to a YA audience."   KLIATT YOUNG ADULT PB BOOK GUIDE

SELF-DEFENSE: A BASIC COURSE
"An eminently practical, concise guide to self-defense...for
young men..."   American Library Association BOOKLIST

"YA - A calm, nonsexist approach to simple yet effective self-
defense techniques...clear photographs...sound advice."
SCHOOL LIBRARY JOURNAL

BRUCE TEGNER'S COMPLETE BOOK OF JUJITSU
"...authoritative and easy-to-follow text..."
SCHOOL LIBRARY JOURNAL

BRUCE TEGNER'S COMPLETE BOOK OF SELF-DEFENSE
Recommended for Y.A. in the American Library Association
BOOKLIST

SELF-DEFENSE & ASSAULT PREVENTION FOR GIRLS & WOMEN (with
Alice McGrath)
"...should be required reading for all girls and women..."
WILSON LIBRARY BULLETIN

"...simple and straightforward with no condescension...easy to
learn and viable as defense tactics..."   SCHOOL LIBRARY JOURNAL

SELF-DEFENSE FOR YOUR CHILD (with Alice McGrath)
[For elementary school-age boys & girls]
"...informative, readable book for family use..."
CHRISTIAN HOME & SCHOOL

DEFENSE TACTICS FOR LAW ENFORCEMENT
"...a practical tool for police academy programs, police programs
at the university level, and for the (individual) officer..."
THE POLICE CHIEF

KUNG FU & TAI CHI: Chinese Karate and Classical Exercise
"...recommended for physical fitness collections."
LIBRARY JOURNAL

SOLO FORMS of Karate, Tai Chi, Aikido & Kung Fu (with Alice McGrath)
"...well-coordinated, step-by-step instructions...carefully captioned
photos...for personal enjoyment and exercise..." YA
American Library Association BOOKLIST

STICK-FIGHTING: SPORT FORMS
"...illustrations and directions are clear and easy to follow...
based on foil fencing, quarterstaff and broadsword...in addition
to sports-oriented use...might prove of value to drama students..."
American Library Association BOOKLIST

RICHARD GENTRY
BETTY GOLDBERG
MIKIO KATSUDA
DELORIS MARSHALL
AARON O'DONNELL
JOE PRADO III
LARRY REYNOSA
DANIEL SCHNEIDER

perform the routines shown in this book.
The authors wish to acknowledge their
contributions and to express gratitude for
their generous participation in the work.

CONTENTS

INTRODUCTION

In many styles of the martial arts, performance of solo or noncompetitive two-man forms is a highly regarded aspect of the activity.

In some specialties of the martial arts, belt degrees are awarded for technical excellence in the demonstration of formal routines. In other specialties, the solo forms are used as warm-ups or as a training exercise, just as shadow boxing is used in boxing. In still other specialties of the martial arts, the solo forms themselves represent the totality of the specialty.

Since this book was designed primarily for the use of those who do not have access to professional instruction, there is no expectation that you would acquire technical perfection by practicing the routines. Rather, the aim is to familiarize you with the general content of formal routines and to offer you an activity for personal enjoyment.

The formal routines of the martial arts are generally presented as rigid, unchangeable, set patterns of sequences of movements from which no deviation is possible. In fact, there are many styles of solo form practice and there is great variety among them. There are choreographed, rehearsed, set routines which are characteristic of Japanese and Korean kata, and there are styles of performance in which variations and improvisations are encouraged.

In this book, several of the routines have been adapted by the performers to suit their individual style of body movement.

One of the routines--the basic form in the Okinawan style-- has been much simplified to allow a beginner to experience the formal movements in their basic components; it is offered here to help those who might have difficulty with a more complex form.

Two of the forms in this text are improvisations. Deloris Marshall's routine, beginning on page 46, and Joe Prado's staff form on page 105 were photographed in the process of being invented.

As a general rule, the more formal the routine, the more emphasis there will be on ceremony. The clothing or uniform in which the classical routines are practiced tend to be more elaborate or prescribed. The etiquette followed in formal routine practice is likely to be more formal as well.

Where both formality and improvisation are encouraged, the routines range from highly elaborate classical forms done in elegant, ornate costumes, to routines done in the equivalent of our jogging outfits.

In China today, both styles of solo forms are widely practiced. A theatrical presentation of varied styles of routines may include classical forms, young and old performers, and routines using standard martial arts movements and gestures, modern adaptations, and even comic inventions.

In the squares and streets of China, individuals and groups can be seen practicing various styles of tai chi in everyday dress. Tai chi is sometimes prescribed as physical therapy.

Throughout Asia, and increasingly throughout the world, people are discovering the satisfactions and benefits of solo movement exercises for flexibility, coordination, body awareness and self-expression.

Convalescents at a sanatorium in Wushi, People's Republic of China, practicing tai chi as physical therapy.

Photo by Alice McGrath

Memorizing the routines can be done in one of two ways--
there is the short-group method and the long-group method.
Using the short-group method, you practice only a few
moves until you feel comfortable doing them. Then you
practice an additional few moves. Then you put those
short sequences together to make a longer sequence. From
there you proceed to practice a few more moves and add
them to your previous sequence, lengthening the series
of moves until finally you have learned all the moves and
perform them as one uninterrupted routine.

The long-group method involves practicing the entire
routine from beginning to end (with as many references
to the photos as you need) and repeating the full routine
until you can do it from memory.

The choice of method will depend on individual preference.
Some people learn better by the long-group and others by
the short-group method.

It is easier to follow the instructions if you face actual
compass points--east, south, west and north. When you
read the instruction to move "forward" or "back," you
are to move forward in the direction you are then facing,
or back from the direction you are facing. The compass
points are constant; "forward" and "back" are relative.

KARATE - TAI KWAN DO (KOREAN) STYLE

This form is characteristic of hard-style karate routines. It is in the general mode of tai kwan do, Korean karate.

Although the movements are fast, the *emphasis* is on strength and power. Each hand and foot blow is highly focused and delivered with strong gestures. The recovery from each action is vigorous. All body movements are perfectly balanced, concentrated and dynamic.

The routine is demonstrated by Daniel Schneider.

1   2

1. Starting position. Stand erect, relaxed, facing east.

2. Bow. Bend forward from the waist only, without lowering your head. Your hands are in front of your chest. Your right hand is fisted, palm out; your open left hand is placed onto the back of your right fist.

3   4

5

3, 4, 5. As you rise from the bow, raise your right knee
without moving your left foot, draw your right foot inward
and deliver a snap kick to the south.

Throughout most of this form your hands are held open,
slightly cupped, with the fingers slightly spread. It is a
relaxed open hand. Except when noted otherwise, your
hand and arm movements flow with the movement of
your upper body.

6   7

6. As you recover, place the ball of your right foot lightly
onto the floor as you fist your right hand and draw it
into your body, and then . . .

7. . . . shift your weight onto your right foot as you deliver
an outward back-knuckle blow with your right hand.

8   9

8, 9. As you pivot on your right foot to face south, draw
your left knee up and deliver a kick to the south.

10

11

12

13

10. Recover with your left foot advanced.

11. Shift your weight onto your left foot as you deliver an outward back-knuckle blow with your left hand and draw your right elbow back.

12, 13, 14. Take a deep step with your right foot, shift your weight back onto your left foot as you draw your right foot up and deliver a snap kick.

16   17

15. As you recover with your right foot advanced, deliver an outward back-knuckle blow with your right fist.

16, 17. Draw your right fist into your body and then deliver a straight out back-knuckle blow.

Pivot on the balls of both feet, turning clockwise to face north.

18

19

20

21

18. Shift your weight onto your right foot. Your left foot is advanced with the toes lightly touching the floor.

19, 20. Raise your left knee and deliver a straight out kick with the bottom of your foot.

21. Recover with your left foot advanced.

Begin to pivot clockwise . . .

22   23

24   25

22, 23. . . . turning to face west. Deliver a kick to the north with your right foot.

24. Without moving your left foot, recover with your upper body turned to the north and your right foot advanced toward the north. Deliver an outward back-knuckle blow with your right fist.

25. Pivoting on your right foot, deliver a high, swinging, sweeping kick to the north with your left foot.

26

27

28

29

26. Recover with your left foot back.

Pivot on your right foot, turning your body to face east, and . . .

27. . . . look north and deliver a high snap kick to the north with your left foot.

28. Recover with your body toward the east. You continue to look toward the north.

29. Pivot on your left foot to face north . . .

30   31

32   33

30. . . . draw your right foot back . . .

31. . . . and deliver a straight out stamping kick.

32. As you recover with your right foot forward, pivot on the balls of both feet . . .

33. . . . to turn your body facing west. Look to the north and deliver an outward back-knuckle blow with your right hand.

34   35   36

37   38

Pivot on your left foot and step around counterclockwise to . . .

34. . . . face south.

35-37. Deliver a high sweeping kick with the outside edge of your left foot.

38. Recover with your left foot back.

39 40 41

42 43

39. Deliver a high toe kick to the east with your left foot.

40-44. Place your kicking foot down behind you and pivot counterclockwise. When you are facing west, deliver a kick to the south with your left foot.

44

45

46

47

48

49

45. As you recover, pivot on your right foot to face south with your weight on your right foot, the ball of your left foot resting lightly on the floor.

46-50. Turning counterclockwise, pivot on your left foot as you raise your right leg and deliver a swinging, sweeping kick.

51. Recover with your right foot back. Your foot points east, your body is turned to the southeast.

52, 53. Deliver a stamping kick to the southeast with your right foot.

54. Recover with your right foot advanced.

50

51

52

53

54

55

56

57

58

55. Deliver an outward back-knuckle blow with your right hand as you draw your left fist back.

Pivot on the balls of both feet, turning counterclockwise . . .

56, 57, 58. . . . to face north and deliver a high snap kick with your left foot.

59

60

61

62

59. Recover with your left foot advanced and deliver an outward back-knuckle blow with your left fist.

60, 61, 62. Deliver a high swinging roundhouse kick with your right foot.

63

64

65

66

63. Recover with your right foot advanced.

Pivoting on your right foot, turn counterclockwise . . .

64, 65, 66. . . . and deliver a high stamping back kick to the northeast with your left foot.

67   68

69   70

67. Recover facing east with your left foot advanced.

68. Stamp straight out with your right foot.

69. Recover into a horse stance, your fists at your sides, palms up.

70. Bow.

KARATE - JAPANESE STYLE

Like the preceding form, this routine is also a hard-style
exercise. A major difference you will note is that hand
blows dominate this form, whereas kicking is primary in
the preceding form.

The gestures are strong, dynamic, and powerful.

At the moment of delivery, the action is fast. Between the
delivery and recovery there is a very slight hesitation; from
recovery to the next action there is a very slight hesitation.
There is a cadence in this routine when it is done properly.
One could imagine performing it to a rhythmic beat or
count.

Richard Gentry demonstrates the form.

71   72   73

71. The starting position. Stand facing east with your
feet slightly apart, your body upright but not rigid, your
open hands at your thighs.

72. The bow. Bend from the waist, looking forward.

73. The position of attention. As you rise, fist both hands.

74

75

76

77

74. As you step to the north with your left foot, bring your left fist to your right shoulder and place your right fist under your left elbow. This is a transition move which continues without hesitation as you . . .

75. . . . turn your upper body to face north, advance your left foot toward the north, block downward with your left forearm, and bring your right fist to your side.

76. As you take a step to the north with your right foot, punch straight out with your right fist and draw your left fist to your side.

77. As you start to turn clockwise by stepping back and around with your right foot, bring your right fist to your left shoulder and your left fist across your body . . .

78

79

80

81

78. . . . and turn your body toward the east. Look south with your right foot pointing south.

79. Block down and outward with your right forearm and draw your left fist into your body.

80. Turn your right fist palm up and . . .

81. . . . draw it to your left shoulder as you draw your left fist cross-body, then . . .

82

83

84

85

86

82. . . . strike back-handed with your right fist as you draw your left fist back.

83. Step clockwise to the south with your left foot as you punch with your left fist and draw your right fist back.

84. Step counterclockwise with your left foot to face east as you . . .

85. . . . draw your left arm cross-body, preparing to . . .

86. . . . block downward with your left arm.

87

88

89

90

91

92

87. Slash/block upward with your left hand.

88. Step forward with your right foot as you slash/block upward with your right hand.

89. Step forward with your left foot as you slash/block upward with your left hand.

90. Step forward with your right foot as you slash/block upward with your right hand.

91. Turning counterclockwise, take a step with your left foot to face north . . .

92. . . . and continue turning to face west, as you prepare to . . .

93   94

95   96   97

93. . . . turn your upper body toward the south and block downward with your left forearm as you draw your right fist to your side.

94. Take a step around and forward (counterclockwise) with your right foot as you deliver a punch with your right fist and draw your left fist to your side.

95. As you begin to pivot counterclockwise . . .

96. . . . to face north, draw your right fist to your left shoulder and draw your left fist cross-body, preparing to . . .

97. . . . block down and outward with your left forearm as you draw your right fist into your body.

98

99

100

101

102

98. Step forward with your right foot as you punch out with your right fist and draw your left fist to your side.

99. Draw your left fist up to your right shoulder as you step . . .

100. . . . to face west and block downward with your left arm as you draw your right fist back.

101. Step forward with your right foot as you punch out with your right fist and draw your left fist back.

102. Step forward with your left foot as you punch with your left fist and draw your right fist back.

103

104

105

106

107

103. Step forward with your right foot as you punch with your right fist and draw your left fist back.

104. Step back and around (counterclockwise) with your left foot as you extend your arms, palms out, and . . .

105. . . . swing your extended arms . . .

106. . . . across your body as you . . .

107. . . . turn your upper body toward the north and . . .

108

109

110   111

108. . . . step to the north with your right foot as you slash high with your right hand and draw your open left hand to your side, palm up.

109. Step to the north with your left foot as you slash high with your left hand and draw your open right hand to your side, palm up.

110. Turn your upper body toward the south as you draw your right hand to your left shoulder and draw your left arm into your body and . . .

111. . . . slash outward with your right hand as you bring your open left hand to your side, palm up.

112

113

114

115

112. Step to the southeast with your left foot as you slash with your left hand and draw your open right hand to your side.

113. As you step around and back (counterclockwise) with your left foot to face east, draw your fists to your sides.

114. Bow.

115. Return to the starting position.

BASIC FORM - OKINAWAN STYLE KARATE

Thrusts of energy alternating with slow, deliberate
movements characterize this short form in the general
style of karate as practiced in Okinawa.

The gesture of each hand blow, block, or stab is vigorous
and sharp. Then there is a brief pause, as though readying
for the next action. The transition movements are slow
but strong, giving the appearance of power under control.

This is an excellent routine for the beginner. Because there
is a minimum of foot movement, all concentration can be
focused on practicing hand and arm techniques.

Aaron O'Donnell performs the routine.

116   117   118

116. Starting position. Face east. Stand erect, but relaxed,
your open hands at your thighs.

117. Bow from the waist, with your head inclined.

118. Rise to the position of attention, your open hands
crossed in front of you.

119   120   121

122   123   124

119. Draw your open hands to your sides.

120. Take a step forward with your right foot, with the toe pointing inward slightly.

121. Make fists.

122. Cross your wrists in front of you.

123. Raise your crossed arms to your chest.

124. Block outward with both arms.

125   126

127   128   129

125. Open your hands.

126. Draw your left open hand back to your side.

127. Thrust upward with your left open hand.

128. As you make a fist of your left hand, draw it back to your side as you punch straight out with your right fist.

129. Open your right hand.

130

131

132 133 134

130. Slash/block outward with both hands.

131. Take a step forward with your left foot, point your toe slightly inward.

132. Fist your left hand.

133. As you draw your right open hand back to your side, palm up, punch out with your left fist.

134. As you open and draw your left hand back to your side, palm up, stab forward with your right hand.

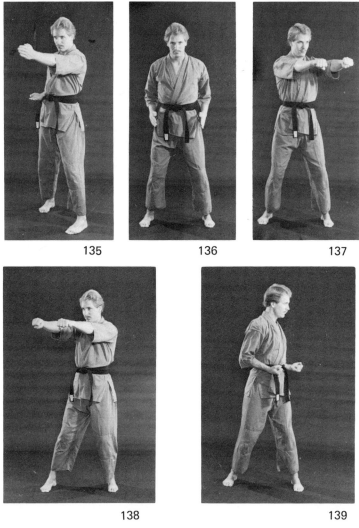

135   136   137

138   139

135. As you draw your right hand back to your side, palm up, stab forward with your left hand.

136. As you step back with your left foot, draw your left hand to your side, both palms toward your body.

137. Without foot movement, turn your upper body to the northeast and punch out with both fists.

138. Without foot movement, turn your upper body to the southeast, draw your fists back and then punch out with both hands.

139. Turn your upper body to the north and draw your fists back to your sides.

140

141

142

143

140. Stab out with your left hand.

141. Open your right hand.

142. Draw your left hand back to your side, both hands palm up.

143. Stab upward with both hands.

144

145

146

147

144. As you draw your right hand back to your side, palm up, bring your left hand cross-body, palm down.

145. Slash up and out with your left hand.

146. As you draw your left hand back to your side, palm up, thrust out with the heel-of-the-palm of your right hand.

147. Turn your upper body to face southeast and thrust out with the heel-of-the-palm of your left hand.

148

149

150

148. Turn your upper body to face northeast and slash with your right hand.

149. Face east as you bring both open hands to your sides.

150. Place your hands at your thighs and bow.

FREE-FORM IMPROVISATION

Before you can improvise in any form--dance, figure
skating, gymnastics or other techniques--you have to learn
basic movement, develop body skills, and practice prearranged routines to develop proficiency.

In addition, improvisation requires imagination and willing-
ness to experiment. Improvisation implies a mode of being
and action which is the direct opposite of the mode of
ritual, traditional performance.

The free-form improvisation which follows consists of
movements taken from karate, dance, and body mechanics.
The style is individual and consistent with the style of the
performer. It is exuberant, graceful, agile, strong, humorous
and intense.

With minimum direction from the authors, the exercise was
improvised in front of the camera, without rehearsal, by
Deloris Marshall.

To perform this exercise as shown:

151. Starting position. Your body is turned to the east,
your left foot points east. Look toward the south. Your
hands are fist-over-fist at your left side. The ball of your
right foot rests lightly on the floor.

152. Without foot movement, raise your left arm over
your head, palm out and raise your right hand to shoulder
height, palm out.

153. Turn your upper body toward the south as you step
south with your right foot. Draw your left fist to your
side, palm up. Your right hand is in a clawing position.

154. Thrust your right hand outward.

155. Step forward with your left foot pointing east.
Look to the east as you draw your right fist to your side
and deliver a back-knuckle blow with your left hand.

156. Stepping counterclockwise with your right foot,
place it on the floor pointing east as you draw your left
fist to your side and deliver a back-knuckle blow with
your right hand.

157. Stepping clockwise with your left foot, place it
forward, pointing east, as you slash forward with your left
hand and draw your right fist to your side.

158. As you raise and open both hands into clawing
position, raise your right knee.

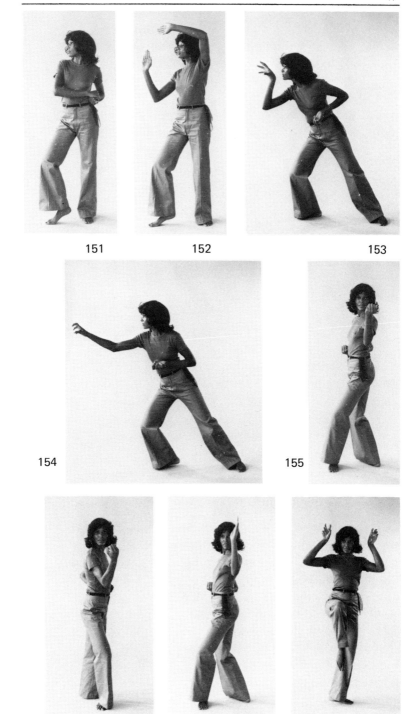

151 152 153

154 155

156 157 158

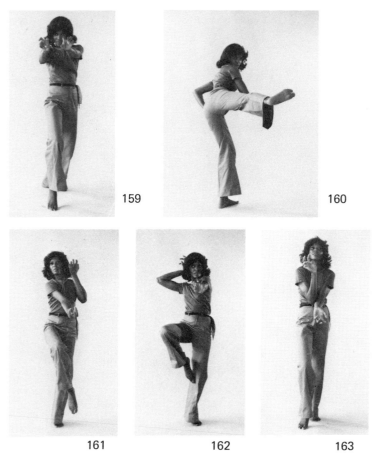

159   160

161   162   163

159. As you take a deep step forward with your right foot, place the ball of the foot lightly on the floor. Thrust out with both clawing hands.

160. As you draw your hands back, deliver a stamping kick with the bottom of your right foot.

161. As you lower your foot, extend your right arm fully with your hand in a clawing position, palm up, and raise your left hand to shoulder height in a clawing position, palm toward you.

162. Place your right foot at your left knee as you stab forward with your left hand and raise your right hand to head height, fingers spread.

163. Place your right foot on the floor, weight resting lightly on the ball of the foot, as you bring your elbows together. Your right hand is raised with the fingers spread, your left hand is lowered, palm up.

164   165

166   167

164. Pushing off from the balls of both feet, deliver a leaping kick with your right foot. When you complete the kick . . .

165. . . . pivot and turn to the north with your right fist drawn to your side and your left fist forward.

Pivot on your right foot to face east.

166. Bring your fisted hands together at your right side as you deliver a stamping kick to the north with your left foot.

167. With your body facing east, deliver two fist blows to the north.

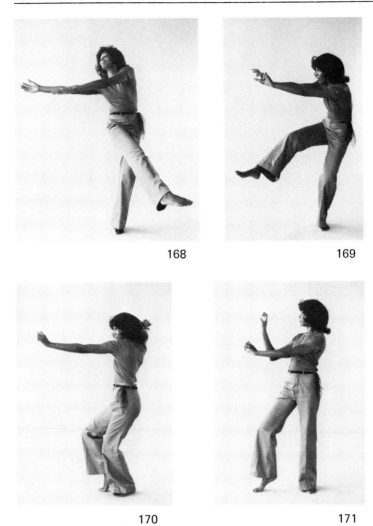

168

169

170

171

168. As you swing your right foot cross-body, swing your arms to the south.

169. Without placing your right foot on the floor, swing your leg clockwise so that you turn facing south.

170. Place the ball of your right foot on the floor slightly in front of your left foot as you thrust outward with your left hand and draw your right hand over your shoulder. Your knees are bent.

171. As you take a short step to the south with your right foot, raise your right hand, palm out, in a clawing position.

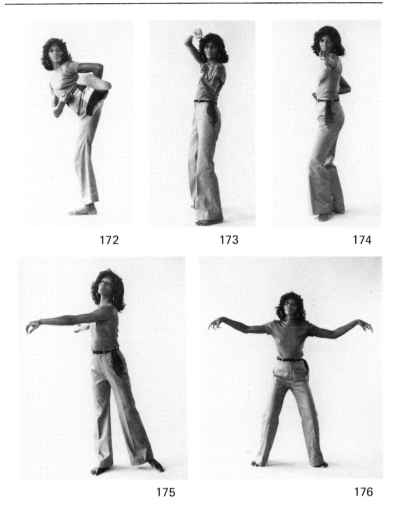

172   173   174

175   176

172. Shift your weight onto your right foot and draw your fists to your sides as you deliver a stamping kick to the east.

173. Place your left foot on the floor so that your body is turned to the south. Look toward the east and raise your right fist to head height; your left fist is forward.

174. Bring your right fist to your side as you punch to the east with your left fist.

175. Extend and swing your arms clockwise as you step counterclockwise with your left foot.

176. Swing your left arm so that both arms are extended outward. Wave your arms several times and then push off from the balls of both feet to . . .

177

178

179

177. . . . leap forward . . .

178. . . . landing with your right foot advanced. Draw your left fist to your side, and raise your right hand in a slashing position.

179. Step forward with your left foot and lower yourself onto your right knee. Draw your right fist to your side and place your open left hand over it.

TAI CHI

The flowing, gentle movements and soft gestures of tai chi scarcely resemble the original hitting and kicking actions from which they evolved. All movement is slow and rounded.

The skilled tai chi performer, with his light, easy steps and smooth transitions, evokes images of moving through a non-resistant medium.

The great circle of tai chi consists of a long routine made up of separate segments, some of which are repeated throughout the routine in a prearranged order. Shown here are the segments which comprise the great circle.

Mikio Katsuda demonstrates the movements.

180   181   182

180. The position of meditation. Stand erect but relaxed, with your head slightly bowed, your hands at your thighs.

181, 182. Raise your arms and begin to inhale, raising your head as . . .

183   184   185

183. . . . your hands rise to your head height. When you have taken the full breath, your hands are palm out.

184. As you begin to exhale slowly, lower your hands as you . . .

185. . . . bend your knees slightly.

186   187

TOUCH THE SOUTH WIND

186. Keeping your left foot in place, start to turn your upper body toward the south, as you begin to move your hands as though around the rim of a wheel . . .

187. . . . and as your hands move around the rim, raise your right knee as your left hand reaches the top of the rim, and then . . .

188

189

188. . . . falls to your side as you raise your right hand to chest height, palm toward you.

189. As you place your right foot on the floor, press gently into the wind with your right forearm as you shift your weight forward.

190   191   192

TOUCH THE EAST WIND

190. As you move your hands back onto the rim of the wheel . . .

191. . . . raise your left knee, and start . . .

192. . . . turning your upper body toward the east.

193   194

193. Your right hand falls to your side as you bring your left arm to your chest height, palm toward you, and as you . . .

194. . . . place your left foot on the floor, press gently into the wind with your left forearm as you shift your weight forward.

THE TIDES

195. Without foot movement, turn your head to look toward the south . . .

196. . . . and raise your right knee and . . .

197. . . . draw your hands in toward your chest as you start to . . .

198. . . . place your right foot on the floor. Extend your arms as though holding a small sphere.

199. Shift your weight back onto your left leg as you draw your hands in toward your chest in the sphere-holding position.

200. Shift your weight onto your right leg and extend your arms with your hands in the sphere-holding position.

201. As you shift your weight back onto your left leg, draw your hands back, palms out.

195   196   197

198   199

200   201

202

203

202. As you shift your weight forward onto your right leg, extend your arms, palms out.

203. Relax your wrists and . . .

204

205

204. . . . as you shift your weight back onto your left leg draw your hands back in the relaxed-wrist position.

205. As you start to shift your weight forward, raise your hands and . . .

206

206. . . . as you extend your arms, raise your hands, palms out.

207

208

THE CRANE

207. As you draw your arms in . . .

208. . . . turn your upper body to face east, and then . . .

209

210

211

212

209. . . . face north as you start to move your hands into the crane position . . .

210. . . . your right arm raised and bent, your right hand forming a beak-like shape. As you start to . . .

211. . . . raise your left knee, bend your left arm.

212. As you place your left foot on the floor and shift your weight forward, your open left hand pushes gently forward.

213   214

215

PERCHING BIRD

213. As you start to turn your upper body clockwise, your arms flow . . .

214, 215. . . . around and outward as you face east. Take a short step with your right foot.

216   217   218

216. Raise your right knee as your arms flow inward, and then . . .

217. . . . swoop down to your left side.

218. As you place your right foot on the floor, touch the inside of your right wrist with your left hand and . . .

219. . . . shift your weight forward.

220   221

VIEW TO THE NORTH

220. As you drop your left hand to your side, you start to turn your upper body to . . .

221. . . . face north, and raise your right arm in front of your forehead, palm down, as you take a step to the north with your left foot, placing weight lightly onto the toe.

222   223

PART THE NORTH WIND

222. Start to draw your left hand up as you . . .

223. . . . raise your left knee and position your hands as though holding the rim of a wheel with your left hand at the top.

224

225

226

227

224-225. As you begin to place your left foot down, lower your left forearm and raise your right hand, preparing to extend the edge of your right hand forward, placing your left heel on the floor as you . . .

226. . . . continue the forward movement with the edge of your hand and place your left foot flat on the floor and . . .

227. . . . shift your weight forward.

228

229

230

231

READY WITH STAFF

228. Shift your weight back . . .

229. . . . onto your right foot as your arms flow outward, and then . . .

230. . . . your arms flow inward as you raise your left knee and . . .

231. . . . position your hands as though holding the rim of a small wheel with your left hand at the top.

232   233

232. As you extend your left leg, draw your bent arms in front of you and . . .

233. . . . as you place your left heel on the floor, lower your hands to the staff-holding position.

STRONG RIGHT FIST

234. As you place your left foot flat on the floor, raise your right hand and lower your left hand.

235. . . . making a circular movement with your hands as you . . .

236. . . . raise your left knee and place your hands in the wheel-holding position.

237. As you prepare to place your foot down, raise and fist your right hand and place your left palm over your right fist.

238. As you place your left foot on the floor, look toward the east and extend your right fist to the east as your left hand drops to your side.

234

235

236

237

238

239   240

FACE THE NORTH WIND

239. As you draw your right fist back, start to take a step to the north with your left foot . . .

240. . . . extending your right fist to the north as you place your foot down, and clasp your right arm with your left hand and shift your weight forward.

SUN WHEEL

241. Turn to face east as you start to raise your arms . . .

242. . . . to make a flowing outward circle . . .

243. . . . up toward your head, and then . . .

244. . . . down in front of your chest, wrists crossed, and continuing . . .

245. . . . gently down to waist level, palms down.

241

242

243

244

245

246

247

248

PLACING THE SPHERE

246. As you step to the north with your left foot, position your hands as though holding a large sphere in front of you.

247. Without foot movement, bring the sphere around to your left side.

248. As you pivot to turn your body toward the east, look toward the southeast and turn the sphere in front of you to bring your left hand to the top and shift your weight onto your bent left leg.

249 250 251

252 253 254

WINGS OPEN AND CLOSE

249, 250. As you shift your weight onto your right leg, your left foot lightly touching the floor, raise your left hand, palm toward you, and shift your weight onto your left leg as you press gently forward with the back of your left hand.

251-253. Draw your right foot back to touch your left foot; step out with your right foot as you raise your right hand in front of your face, palm toward you and lower your left hand, palm down. Your left heel rests on the floor.

254. Draw your left foot back as you raise your left hand, palm toward you, touching the floor lightly with the tip of your left foot. Drop your right hand, palm up.

255   256

THE SERPENT DESCENDS

255. Continue drawing your left foot back until it touches
your right leg as you raise your right hand.

256. Without moving your right foot, bend your right knee
and shift your weight back onto your right leg. Turn your
upper body to the north, extending your left leg to the north.
Your right arm is raised and bent, with the wrist relaxed.
Your left arm is bent and extended with your left hand
palm up.

257

258

259

THE STORK

257. Rise and shift your weight onto your left leg as you start to . . .

258. . . . raise your arms and your right knee until you are . . .

259. . . . standing on your left leg, with your right knee raised. Your right hand is raised with the fingers spread. Your left hand drops to your side.

260

261

262

263

PLUCK THE BLOSSOM

260. Place your right foot on the floor and . . .

261. . . . shift your weight onto your right leg as you raise your left knee and draw your right arm up and back.

262. Place the tip of your left foot lightly on the floor and . . .

263. . . . bend your right knee and curl your back as you place your right hand close to your left foot. Your left hand lightly touches your right elbow.

264   265

266   267

DANCING BEAR

264. As you rise, shift your weight onto your left leg and lift your right knee and extend both arms outward.

265. Extend your right leg, your toes pointing up. Raise both hands, palms outward, and as you . . .

266. . . . step down onto your right foot, lower your hands to your sides.

267. As you raise your left knee, your arms flow upward . . .

268   269

268. . . . and your left leg is extended.

269. Place your left heel lightly on the floor.

SUPPLICATION

270. As you place the tip of your left foot on the floor, draw your arms in toward your body and place them in the position of holding a small sphere.

271, 272. As you shift your weight forward onto your left leg, extend your arms fully with your hands in the sphere-holding position.

273, 274. As you shift your weight back onto your right leg, cross your arms and . . .

275. . . . bring your crossed arms in front of your chest, palms toward you. The tip of your left foot touches the floor lightly.

270

271

272

273

274

275

276

277

278

TERMINUS

276. Turn to face east. Your head is slightly bowed.
Your hands are relaxed at your thighs.

277. As you raise your head, inhale and raise your extended
arms, keeping your wrists relaxed.

278. Open your hands, palms out . . .

279

280

281

279, 280. . . . lowering your arms as you bow your head and exhale.

281. The ending position is with your head slightly bowed and your relaxed hands at your thighs.

STYLIZED TAI CHI

An adaptation of classical tai chi is shown here. This is not an improvisation; it is an expression of individual body movement applied to a formal routine. Although the performer executes some of the same movements and gestures as shown in the preceding section, her personal style is apparent.

The mode of movement is the same as in the previous routine. It is a complete form as shown.

Betty Goldberg adapted and here performs the exercise.

282   283   284

282. Starting position. Face east. Your body is upright but relaxed; your hands are at your thighs. Inhale.

283. Drop your head slightly as you exhale.

284. As you raise your head, cross your arms with your hands at your shoulders, your left arm over your right arm.

285. As you take a step to the southeast with your right foot, raise your left arm with your wrist relaxed, as your right arm drops gently to your side, palm forward.

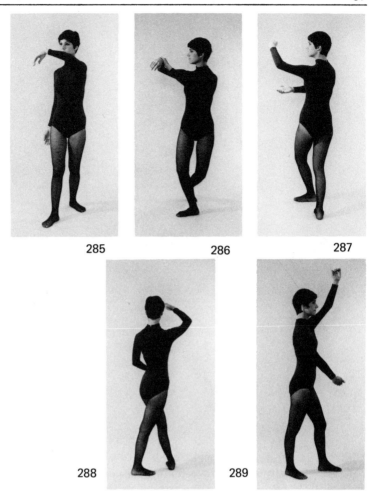

285   286   287

288   289

286. Raise your right hand and place it under your left palm as you position the tip of your left foot behind your right foot.

Turning clockwise, swing your left leg around as you pivot on your right foot. Your left foot points toward the south. Your right foot is positioned behind your left foot.

287. As you turn, raise your left arm, wrist relaxed. Your right hand drops gently to your side.

288. Pivot on both feet to face west as you raise your right arm and drop your left arm, and . . .

289. . . . pivot on the balls of both feet, turning clockwise to face north. Your hands are placed as though holding the rim of a large wheel with your left hand at the top.

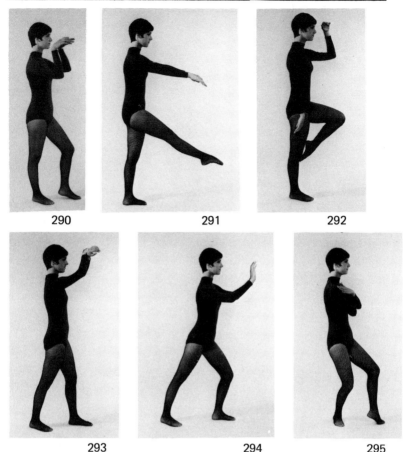

290   291   292

293   294   295

290. As you shift your weight back onto your right foot
with the ball of your left foot resting lightly on the floor,
draw your hands in front of your face, wrists relaxed.

291. Shift your weight onto your left leg, extend your
right leg and extend both arms fully, palms down.

292. As you place your right foot on the floor and shift
your weight onto it, lower your right hand to your side
and raise your left hand in front of your face. Touch your
right knee with your left foot.

293. As you step onto your left foot, raise both hands to
your head height, wrists crossed.

294. As you shift your weight forward and bend your left
knee, push outward with the palms of both hands.

295. Shift your weight back onto your right leg with the
ball of your left foot resting lightly on the floor. Cross
your hands at your chest and begin to . . .

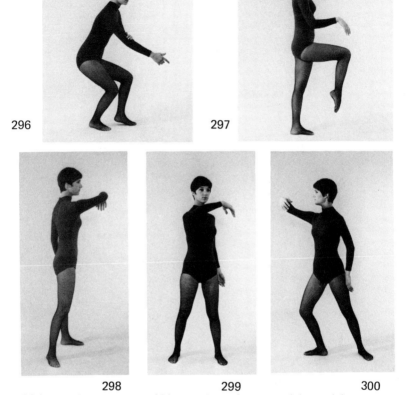

296

297

298 299 300

296. . . . lower yourself into a bent-knee position with your right hand extended, the index finger pointing downward and your left hand resting lightly at your right arm.

297. As you rise, shift your weight onto your left leg and raise your right knee. Your left hand is raised and bent at your head height, wrist relaxed. Your right hand is held over your right knee with your wrist relaxed . . .

298. As you place your right foot on the floor, your left hand drops gently to your side as you raise your right arm and begin to . . .

299. . . . turn, stepping clockwise with your left foot. Your raised arm moves with a sweeping, flowing motion as you continue to . . .

300. . . . turn clockwise to face south. Shift your weight onto your right leg. Push gently with the back of your right hand.

301   302

303   304

301. As you shift your weight onto your left leg, raise
your right knee and extend your right arm, palm toward you.

302. As you place your right foot on the floor, extend both
arms and position your hands as though holding a small
sphere with your left hand at the top.

303. Take a step with your left foot and turn your right
hand palm down, wrist relaxed. Place your left hand lightly
at your right arm.

304. Pivoting on the balls of both feet, turn your body to
the west. Look to the north. Your left hand drops to your
side. Your right arm flows around in an arc, your palm
toward you.

305   306   307

308   309

305. Moving clockwise, step to the northwest with your right foot. Raise and extend your left arm and place your right hand gently at your left wrist. Continue moving clockwise as you . . .

306. . . . take a step with your left foot so that you are facing north. Your left heel rests on the floor. Your arms begin to move into position as though . . .

307. . . . your hands are holding the rim of a large wheel with your right hand at the top. Raise your left knee.

308. As you place the ball of your left foot on the floor, your bent left arm is held at head height, palm down, and your right hand is held under your left elbow, palm down.

309. As you shift your weight onto your left leg, raise your right leg and extend both arms to the side. Moving clockwise . . .

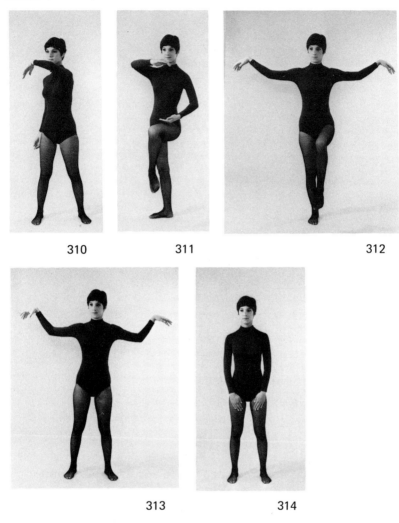

310   311   312

313   314

310. . . . swing your right leg and place your foot on the ground so that you face east. Your right arm drops to your side.

311. Raise your left knee as your hands move into position as though holding the rim of a wheel, your right hand at the top.

312. As you start to place your foot down, raise both arms outward and make several waving motions with your arms as you stand with your weight equally distributed on both feet.

314. Allow your hands to drop gently to your thighs, as in the starting position.

KUNG FU - THE LITTLE DRAGON FORM

This adaptation of a classical kung fu form is distinguished by the style and variety of the techniques and by stylized body gestures. Kung fu forms are traditionally taught with reference to the "attack" and the "opponent."

The routine simulates a situation in which the "opponent" and the performer move back and forth, attacking and defending and counterattacking. The little dragon punches, claws, kicks, grabs, uses takedowns, and simulates an escape from a hold.

The style of movement alternates between whipping and slashing hand blows to power punching--from snapping circle foot blows to stamping kicks.

Joe Prado III performs the routine.

315   316   317

Starting position. Face east, standing erect, with your feet close together.

315. Bow. Your head is slightly inclined. The palm of your left hand covers your right fist which is held at chest height.

316. Rise to a position of attention with your hands in front of you, left palm over right hand.

317. Step counterclockwise with your left foot to assume a side horse stance. Your body is turned toward the north, you look toward the east. Your knees are slightly bent, your feet are shoulder width apart.

318   319   320

321   322   323

318. Punch to the east with your right fist.

319. Punch to the east with your left fist.

320. As you shift your weight back onto your left foot, draw your fists back and deliver a snap kick with your right foot as though to block a low kick . . .

321. . . . recover to the side horse stance and counter with a right punch.

322. In response to the capture of your right arm by the opponent . . .

323. . . . punch with your left fist and simulate breaking the hold by thrusting down sharply with your right elbow.

324

325

326

327

324. Counterattack by simulating grabbing the opponent with both hands and . . .

325. . . . pull him forward as you deliver a knee kick.

326. Recover with your right foot advanced and then . . .

327. . . . shift your weight back onto your left foot to deliver a kick with your right foot.

328. Recover with your right foot advanced and start to . . .

328

329

330

331

332

329, 330. . . . catch your opponent's leg, simulate application of a hold, and . . .

331. . . . simulate taking him to the ground.

332. Block with your left arm as though to deflect a kick from the opponent on the ground. Your left hand is in a guard position.

333. As the opponent rises, kick with your right foot, and . . .

334. . . . punch with your right hand.

335. As the opponent kicks, you catch his ankle with your right hand, and . . .

336, 337. . . . carry it to your right side as you topple him to the ground by levering up with your right hand as you press at his shoulder with your left hand.

333

334

335

336

337

338

339

340

341

338. As he rises, kick with your right foot.

339. Punch with your right fist.

340. Parry with your left arm as though deflecting a hand blow.

341. Counter with an elbow blow with your right arm, and . . .

342

343

344

345

342. . . . deliver a whipping back-handed slash with your left hand, followed by a . . .

343. . . . palm-up cross-body slash with your left hand, followed by . . .

344. . . . an upward stabbing blow with your left hand.

345,346. Simulate a grab with your left hand as you start to position your leg . . .

346

347   348

347, 348. . . . for a back sweeping-leg trip to take your
opponent down. The opponent is defeated.

349   350

349. You rise with your hands palms forward.

350. Bow.

AIKIDO-STYLE STAFF KATA

This form is a series of thrusting, striking and blocking moves, simulating defensive actions against an attack. Kata is one of the ways to practice to achieve skill in handling the staff as a defense against single or multiple opponents.

The staff is held firmly enough for complete control, but with a light grasp for easy transition from one movement to the next.

Body movements and gestures are flowing, graceful, smooth, and continuous. But the positive actions -- the thrusts, blocks and strikes -- are performed vigorously, with focused energy.

Larry Reynosa performs the kata.

351   352

THIRTEEN-MOVEMENT KATA

FIRST MOVEMENT

351. The starting position. Your body is erect, your left foot advanced; your right foot is at an angle. Your left hand holds the staff about three inches from the top. The staff is positioned into the "Y" of your right hand and braced onto the floor.

352. As you slide forward on the ball of your left foot, raise the staff with your right hand as you thrust it forward across the palm of your left hand and draw your right hand toward you. The staff is horizontal to the floor.

353   354

355   356

SECOND MOVEMENT

353. Raise your right hand to your head level and position the "Y" of your left hand under the staff.. . .

354. . . . and block overhead as you prepare to . . .

355. . . . step with your right foot and slide your right hand toward your left hand . . .

356. . . . and rotate the staff as you step forward with your right foot. Your right hand is now in front of your left hand.

357

THIRD MOVEMENT

357. Making an arcing movement forward, rotate the staff as you slide your right hand back, raise the staff and then strike down.

358

359

FOURTH MOVEMENT

358. Raise your left hand . . .

359. . . . blocking upward. The staff is in the "Y" of both hands. Your right hand is at your eye level.

360   361

360. Shift your weight back and then . . .

361. . . . as you slide your right foot forward, draw the
point of the staff around to your right side, then overhead,
and then thrust down and forward in one circular, smooth
motion. The point is slightly raised at the completion of
this movement.

FIFTH MOVEMENT

362. Shift your weight forward onto your right foot as
you raise your left hand and block. The blocking action
continues through photo 366.

363. With your right foot in place, step forward with your
left foot . . .

364. . . . pivot in place and turn 180° clockwise, and . . .

365. . . . take a step back with your right foot, and . . .

366. . . . reverse your hand position so that your right hand
is above the left hand. This action rotates the staff. Your
right hand grasps the staff in a reverse grip, the thumb down.

362   363   364

365   366

367   368

SIXTH MOVEMENT

367. As you step with your right foot, relax your right hand grip on the staff, preparing to . . .

368. . . . regrip with a natural grip and shift your weight forward as you strike downward.

369 370

SEVENTH MOVEMENT

369. Pivot on the ball of your right foot, turn 180° counterclockwise, and . . .

370. . . . continue the counterclockwise turn, sliding your left foot behind you, and block to guard the left side of your head.

371

EIGHTH MOVEMENT

371. Thrust straight out, arms and staff fully extended.

372   373

NINTH MOVEMENT

372. Pivot on the balls of both feet, turn counterclockwise as you slide your right hand back . . .

373. . . . and as you shift your body weight forward onto your left foot, thrust the staff straight out.

TENTH MOVEMENT

374. Turning clockwise, pivot on your right foot . . .

375. . . . as you start to bring the staff around to your right side, and begin to step around . . .

376. . . . 180° with your left foot and block to guard the right side of your head.

ELEVENTH MOVEMENT

377. Shift your weight back onto your right foot as you raise the staff to eye level, in position to . . .

378. . . . thrust it straight out as you shift your body weight forward.

374

375

376

377

378

379

380

TWELFTH MOVEMENT

379. Drawing your left foot back, position the staff upright in front of you, your right hand below the left.

380. Draw the staff back at your right side and deliver a downward block.

381

382

THIRTEENTH MOVEMENT

381. Step forward with your left foot, thrusting the staff out.

382. Ending position. The staff is held lightly touching the floor just in front of your left foot, hands as shown.

KUNG FU STAFF - FREE-FORM EXERCISE

Improvisation is encouraged in many Chinese styles of the martial arts. The ability to perform classical, rehearsed, choreographed routines, and the ability to improvise are both ranked as necessary skills to develop the highest levels of achievement.

Practice of formal routines develops technical skill and dexterity in handling and controlling the staff. Improvisation allows for development of individual style, flexibility and creativity.

The following free-form exercise was improvised by Joe Prado III.

383

383. The starting position. Standing erect but relaxed, he holds the staff with both hands, as shown. The staff has no recognizable point or butt. In order to describe the actions, the forward tip of the staff will be called the "point" and the rear-facing tip will be called the "butt." Either end of the staff can be point or butt.

384

385

386

387

384-386. He rotates the stick clockwise and simulates striking forward with the point.

387-389. He rotates the staff with his right hand and grasps the butt with his left hand and continues to rotate the staff in position to strike downward with the point.

390. He raises the point of the staff and strikes a whipping blow outward.

391. He grasps the staff at both ends and simulates a blocking action to his right side, then . . .

392. . . . simulates a block against a low blow from the same direction, squatting as he blocks.

393. He rises and draws the butt of the staff back and . . .

388

389

390

391

392

393

394

395

396

397

398

399

394. . . . strikes a forward jabbing blow with the point.

395. He draws the staff back and rotates it with his left hand, then . . .

396. . . . transfers the staff to his right hand. He rotates it with one hand and then . . .

397, 398. . . . delivers a downward whipping blow with the point.

399. He raises the staff and strikes downward.

400   401   402

403   404   405

400. As he raises the point of the stick, he crouches and blocks.

401. He rises and thrusts forward with the point of the staff and then . . .

402. . . . draws both hands to the butt end and strikes backhanded.

403. He grasps the tip of the staff with his left hand and blocks to his right side.

404. He transfers the staff to his right hand.

405. He completes the routine with the stick held as shown, his left hand palm outward.

INDEX

BRUCE TEGNER WAS BORN IN Chicago in 1929. Both his parents were professional teachers of judo and jujitsu.

In a field in which most individuals concentrate on a narrow specialty, Bruce Tegner's experience was unusual. His education covered many aspects of weaponless fighting of many styles as well as sword and stick techniques. At the age of twenty-one, after becoming California state judo champion, he devoted himself to research, course development, teaching and teacher-training.

ALICE McGRATH has been teaching, researching and writing in the field of the martial arts since 1957 and is a consultant to Encyclopedia Americana.

BRUCE TEGNER & ALICE McGRATH collaborated on course development for physical education classes, conducted scores of workshops, lecture/demonstrations and in-service training programs for teachers throughout the country. The innovative methods which they introduced into the field were highly controversial at the time they were originally presented, but have come to be widely accepted as being consistent with modern concepts of health and physical education.

FOR A FREE DESCRIPTIVE BROCHURE
describing our complete line of BRUCE TEGNER
books on karate, judo, self-defense, kung fu,
tai chi and other specialty titles in this field,
as well as ELLEN KEI HUA'S inspirational
books, write to:

THOR PUBLISHING COMPANY
P.O. Box 1782
Ventura, CA 93002